Look at Me I'm Learning Arabic
(A STORY FOR AGES 3-6)

By Daniel Williamson

Illustrated by Kleverton Monteiro

First published in 2019 by Daniel Williamson
www.danielwilliamson.co.uk
This edition published in 2020
Text © Daniel Williamson 2019
Illustrations © Kleverton Monteiro 2019
Cover design © by Uzuri Designs 2019

Translation by Mahmoud Elsebaei

All rights reserved. No part of this publication may be reproduced, stored in a retrieval system or transmitted, in any form or by any means, electronic, mechanical, photocopying, recording or otherwise, without the prior permission of the copyright holder.

ISBN 978-1-913583-03-3

www.danielwilliamson.co.uk

This book is dedicated
to my daughter
Carmela

I'm a small person in a big, big world!

أَنَا شَخْصٌ صَغيرٌ، أَعيشُ فِي عالِمٍ كَبيرٍ جِدًّا.

anā shkhsun sghyrun , a'eyshu fy 'ealmen kbyren jdan.

I know people bigger than me. Bigger people know more things because they start to learn when they are small.

أَعْرِفُ أَشْخَاصَ أَكْبَرَ مِنِّي، الكِبارُ يَعْرِفونَ أَشْياءَ أَكْثَرَ لِأَنَّهُم بَدَأُوا التَّعَلُّمَ وَهُم صِغارٌ.

a'erfu ashkhas akbr mny, alkibaru y'erfwn ashya' akthr lanhum bdauwa alt'elum whum sgharun.

Not everyone speaks English like me. Some bigger people speak Arabic, some speak two languages!

لَيْسَ كُلُّ النّاسِ يَتَحَدَّثُونَ الإِنْكِلِيزِيَّةَ مِثْلِي، بَعْضُ الكِبارِ يَتَحَدَّثُونَ العَرَبِيَّةَ، وَ بَعْضُهُمْ يَتَحَدَّثُ لُغَتانِ.

lys kulu alnas ythdthuwn alenklyzyh mthly, b'edu alkbar ythdthuwn al'erbyh, wb'eduhum ythdthu lughtan,

I want to learn Arabic too so I can speak to Arabic speaking people and make even more friends!

.أُرِيدُ أَنْ أَتَعَلَّمَ العَرَبِيَّةَ أَيْضًا حَتَّى أَسْتَطِيعَ التَّحَدُّثَ مَعَ العَرَبِ وَيَكُونُ لَدَيَّ أَصْدِقاءُ أَكْثَرَ

aurydu an at'elm al'erbyh aydan hta astty'e alta hduth m'e al'erb wykuwnu ldy asdqa'u akthr.

First I'm going to learn to count using the peas on my plate.
أَوَّلًا سَوْفَ اتَّعَلَمُ العَدُّ بِاسْتِخْدَامِ حَبَّاتِ البازلاء فِي صَحْنِي
awlan swf at'elmu al'edu bastkhdam hbat albazela' fy shny

ONE
واحِدٌ
wahdun

TWO
اثْنانِ
athnan

THREE
ثَلاثَةٌ
thlathtun

FOUR
أَرْبَعَةٌ
arb'etun

FIVE
خَمْسَةٌ
khmstun

SIX
سِتَّةٌ
sitatutn

SEVEN
سَبْعَةٌ
sb'etun

EIGHT
عَشْرَةٌ
thmanytun

NINE
تِسْعَةٌ
ts'etun

TEN
عَشْرَةٌ
'eshrtun

Now I know how to count to ten! Look at me
I'm learning Arabic, learning Arabic is Fun!

اَلَانِ اعْرِفْ كَيْفَ أَعُدُّ اِلَّى عَشَرَة، اُنْظُروا اَلِي وَانَا اَتَّعَلْمُ العَرَبِيَّةَ ، تَعَلُّمُ العَرَبِيَّةِ مُمْتِعٌ !

alan a'erf kyf a'ed ala 'eshrh, aunzurwa aly wana at'elm al'erbyh ,
t'elum al'erbyh mumt'eun !

I wonder what to say if I meet a Arabic speaking person? I think I would say - "Hello, how are you?" Then they would say - "I'm fine thanks and you?"

يَا تَرَى مَاذَا أَقُولُ عِنْدَمَا الْتَقِي شَخْصاً يَتَحَدَّثُ العَرَبِيَّةَ؟ أَظُنُّ انَّنِي أَقُولُ "مَرْحَبًا، كَيْفَ حالُكَ؟". ثُمَّ يَرُدُّ عَلَي وَ يَقُولُ "أَنَا بِخَيْرٍ وَ اَنْتَ كَيْفَ حالُكَ؟"

ya tra madha aqwlu 'endma altqy shkhsun ythdthu al'erbyh? adhunu anny aqwlu – " mrhban, kyf haluk?". thum yrudu 'ely w yquwlu – " ana bkhyren w ant kyf haluk?"

Then I would need to tell them my name. I would say –
"Hello, my name is _____, what's your name?"

ثُمَّ بَعْدَ ذَلِكَ سَأَخْبِرُهُ بِاسْمِي ، سَأَقُولُ لهُ " مَرْحَبًا، اسْمِي ـــــــــ.وَأَنْتَ مَا اسْمُكَ ؟"

thumˉ bʾedˑ dhalk saḵhbruhu besmẏ , saquwlu lhu –
" mrhban , asmẏ____ wantˉ maˉ asmuk ?"

Now I want to tell them my age and ask how old they are.
Let's see if I can remember the numbers!

وَالَانِ اِرِيدَ اَنْ أَخْبَرَهُ كَمْ عُمْرِي وَاسْأَلُهُ كَمْ عُمْرُهُ ، هَيَّا نَرَى إِذَا كُنتُ أَتَذَكَّرُ الاَرْقَامَ

waĪan arydu an ukhbr̄hu kmā 'eumr̄y wasaĪhu kmā 'eumr̄uhu,
hyā nr̄ā edhā kunt̊ atdhk̄ru alarqam̄

ONE	TWO	THREE	FOUR	FIVE	SIX	SEVEN	EIGHT	NINE	TEN
وَاحِدٌ	اثْنَانِ	ثَلَاثَةٌ	أَرْبَعَةٌ	خَمْسَةٌ	سِتَّةٌ	سَبْعَةٌ	ثَمَانِيَةٌ	تِسْعَةٌ	عَشْرَةٌ
wahdun	athnan	thlathtun	arb'etun	khmstun	Sitatutn	sb'etun	thmanytun	ts'etun	'eshrtun

I am _____ years old, how old are you?

عُمْرِي _____ سَنَةً ، وَأَنْتَ كَمْ عُمُرُكَ ؟

'eumry ____ sanh , want km 'eumuruk?

Look at me I'm learning Arabic!
Learning Arabic is fun!

اُنْظُروا اَلي وَانَا اتَّعَلَّمُ العَرَبِيَّة ، تَعَلُّمُ العَرَبِيَّة مُمْتِعٌ !

Aundhurwa aly wana at'elm al'erbyh,
t'elumu al'erbyh mumt'eun!

I need to know how to say the things I like and the things I don't like, let's try some sentences!

أَحْتاجُ اَنْ أَتَعَلَّمُ كَيْفَ أُعْبِرَ عَنْ الأَشْياءِ الَّتي أَحَبُّها وَالَّتي لَا أَحَبُّها، هَيّا نُجَرِّبُ بَعْضَ الجُمَلِ !

ahtaju an at'elmu kyf au'ebur 'en alashya'ِ alty ahbuha walty la ahubha, hya nujrbu b'ed aljuml !

I like sunny days. I like to go to the park
and play on the slide and swings!

أَحَبُّ الأَيَّامَ المُشَمَّسَةَ، أَحَبُّ الذَّهابَ اِلَى المُتَنَزَّهِ واللَّعِبَ بِالْأُرْجوحَةِ والتَّزَحْلُقِ!

ahbu alayam almushmsah, ahbu aldhab ala almutnzh
wall'eb balaurjwhh waltzhluq!

I also love playing with my friends outside.
Sometimes we play football, sometimes we play hide and seek!

أَيْضًا أَحَبُّ اللَّعِبَ مَعَ أَصْدِقَائِي فِي الْخَارِجِ ، أَحْيَانًا نَلْعَبُ كُرَةَ القَدَمِ ،
وَأَحْيَانًا نَلْعَبُ الغَمِيضَةَ !

Aydan ahbu allʼeb mʼe asdqaʼey fy alkharjj, ahyanan
nlʼebu kurat alqadm, wahyanana nlʼebu alghmydh !

I don't like when it's rainy and windy so I go to the cinema, watch cartoons and eat popcorn.

لَا أُحِبُّ الْجَوَّ الْمُمْطِرَ شَدِيدَ الرِّياحِ وَلِذَا أَذْهَبُ اِلَى السِّينَما أُشاهِدُ الأَفْلام المُتَحَرِّكَةَ وَأَكْلَ اَلْفَشارَ

la auhbu aljaw almumtr shdyd alryah wldha adhahbu ala alsynma aushahdu alaflam almutahrkah wakul alfishar!

My favourite thing to do is go for a picnic.
I like eating apple slices but I prefer bananas!

أَمَّا الشَّيْءُ المُفَضَّلُ عِنْدِي فَهُوَ الذَّهابُ فِي رِحْلَةٍ ، احبُ اكَلَ شَرائِحِ التُّفَّاحِ لكِنِّي افَضِلُ المَوْزِ

ama alshy'u almufdlu 'endy fhuw aldhihabu fy rhlten,
ahbu akl shra'eh altufah lakny ufadlu almawz !

Last time I went to the park I saw a huge rainbow.
Let's see if I can remember all the colours!

أَخَرَ مُرَّةٍ ذَهَبْتُ اِلَّى الْمُتَنَزَّه رَأَيْتُ قَوْسَ قُزَح عِمْلاقٍ، دَعونا
نَرَى اَنْ كُنْتَ أَتَذَكَّرُ كُلَّ الأَلْوَاَنِ !

aukhrᵃ murtin dhḇutᵘ aĺa almutnẕh rayutᵘ qwsᵒ quzhē
'emĺaqen, dᵉewna nrā anᵓ kuntᵘ atdhākrū kulᵒ alal̄wan !

RED	الأَحْمَرُ alahmru
ORANGE	وَالْبُرْتُقَالِيُّ walburtuqalyu
YELLOW	وَالأَصْفَرُ walasfru
GREEN	وَالأَخْضَرُ walakhdru
BLUE	وَالأَزْرَقُ walazrqu
INDIGO	وَالْنِيلِي walnyly
VIOLET	وَالْبَنَفْسَجِيُّ walbnfsjyu

The colours of the rainbow are red, orange, yellow, green, blue, indigo and violet!

أَلْوانُ قَوْسِ قُزَحٍ هِيَ الأَحْمَرُ وَالْبُرْتُقَالِيُّ وَالأَصْفَرُ وَالأَخْضَرُ وَالأَزْرَقُ وَالنِّيلِي وَالْبَنَفْسَجِيُّ!

alwanu qws quzhen hy alahmru walburtuqalyu walasfru walakhdru walazrqu walnyly walbnfsjyu !

Look at me I'm learning Arabic!
Learning Arabic is fun!

! اُنْظُروا اَلي وَانَا اتَّعَلَمُ العَرَبِيَّة ، تَعَلُّمُ العَرَبِيَّة مُمْتِعٌ

aundhurwa aly wana at'elm al'erbyh ,
t'elumu al'erbyh mumt'eun!

At home I have some different pets and they are different colours too! I have a brown dog, a black and white cat and a grey rabbit.

فِي بَيْتِي بَعْضِ الحَيَوَانَاتِ الأَلِيفَةِ ، لَدَيَّ كَلْبُ بَنِي اللَّوْنِ وَقَطُّ لَوْنُهُ أَبْيَضُ وَأَسْوَدُ وَأَرْنَبُ لونه رَمادِيٌّ

fy byty b'ed alhywanat alalyfah , ldy klbu bunny allawn wqitun lwnuhu abydu waswd warnbun lwnuhu ramadyun !

My dog likes me to throw his ball for him,
he always brings it back, it's his favourite game!

يُحِبُّ الكَلْبُ أَنْ أَلْقَى لهُ الكُرَةَ وَدَائِمًا مَا يَسْتَطِيعُ اِرِّجاعَها ، هَذِهِ لعبته المُفَضَّلَةُ!

yuhbu alklbu an ulqi lahu alkurh wda'emana ma ystty'eu arja'eha ,
hdhi lu'ebthu almufdalh !

My cat likes to sleep on the sofa all day,
he's a very lazy cat!

وَالْقَطُّ يُحِبُّ أَنْ يَنامَ عَلَى الأَرِيكَةِ طَوالَ اليَوْمِ ، انه كَسولٌ جِدًّا!

walqitu yuhbu an ynam 'ela alarykh twal alywm,
enhu kswlun jdan!

My rabbit lives in the garden, he eats carrots all day, they help him see better at night time!

أَمَّا الأَرْنَبُ فَيَعِيشُ فِي الحَدِيقَةِ ، يَأْكُلُ الجُزَرَ طَوَالَ اليَوْمِ ، فَالْجُزُرُ يُسَاعِدُهُ عَلَى الرُّؤْيَةِ بِشَكْلٍ أَفْضَلَ اثْنَاءِ اللَّيْلِ

amā alarnbu fyʿeyshu fy alhdyqah , yakulu aljazr twal alywm , faljuzuru yusaʿeduhu ʿelā alruʿeyh bshklen afḍl athnāʾ allyl !

At night time I get into my pyjamas, I love getting into bed for a story, then I close my eyes and slowly fall asleep, ready to learn more Arabic tomorrow...

فِي المَساءِ ، ارْتَدَي مَلابِسَ النَّوْمِ ، أَحَبُّ الاسْتِماعَ الَى قِصَّةَ قَبْلَ النَّوْمِ ، ثُمَّ أَغْمِضُ عَيْنِي وِانامَ بِبَطيءٍ ، وَاسْتَعَدَّ لِتَعَلُّمِ المَزيدِ مِنَ العَرَبِيَّةِ فِي اليَوْمِ التَّالِي

fy almsa', artdy mlabis alnwm, ahbu alastma'e ala qisah qabl alnwm, thum ughmdu 'eyny w'anam bbty'en, wast'ed lt'elum almzyd mn al'erbyh fy alywm altaly

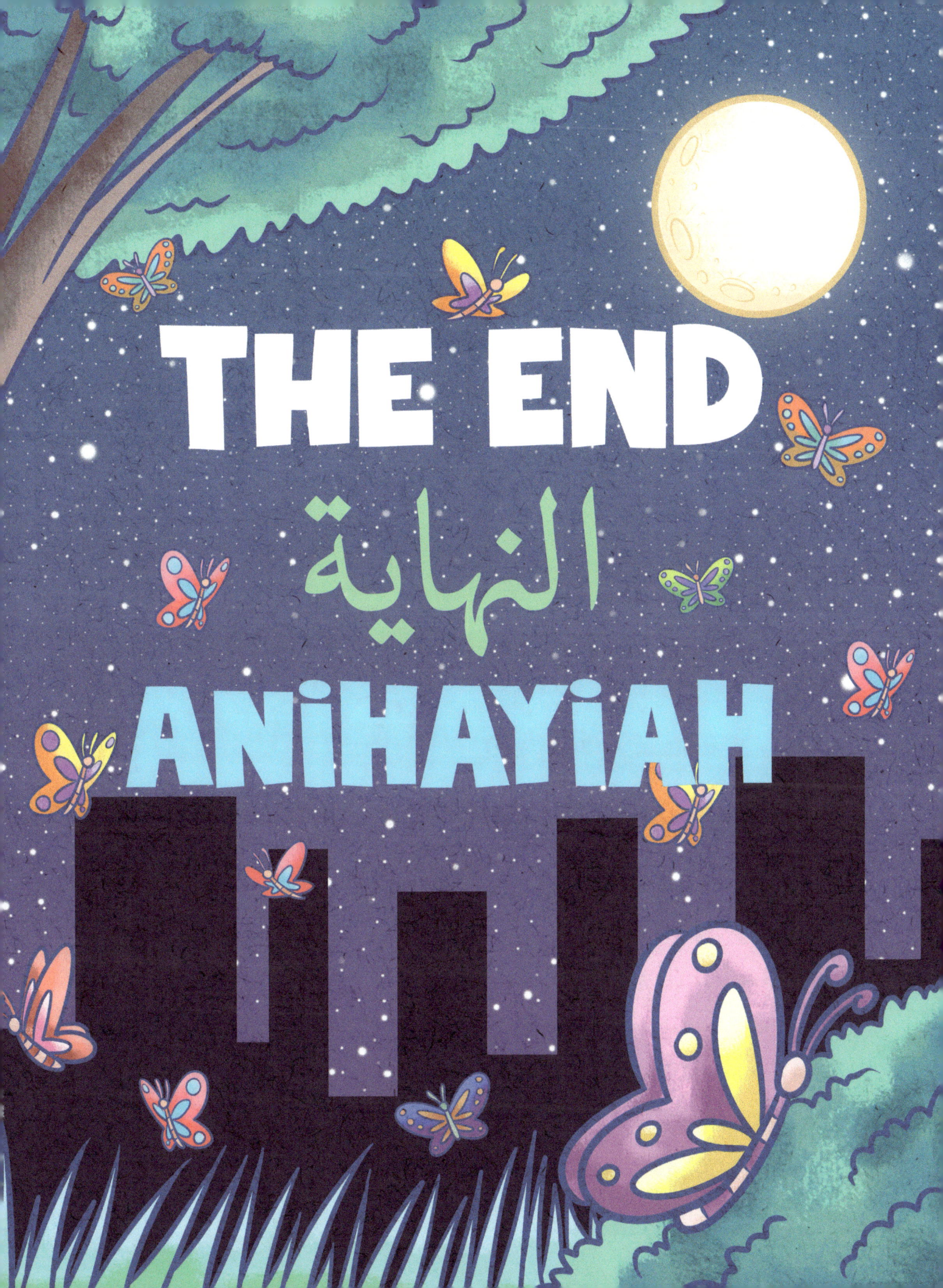

This author has developed a bilingual book series designed to introduce children to a number of new languages from a very young age.

If you enjoyed reading this story, you will undoubtedly like popular rhyming picture books from this author which are also currently available.

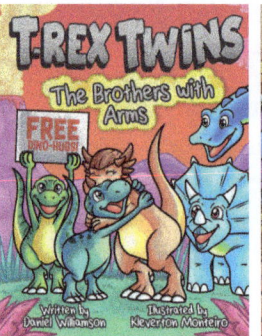
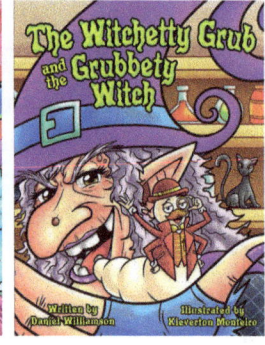
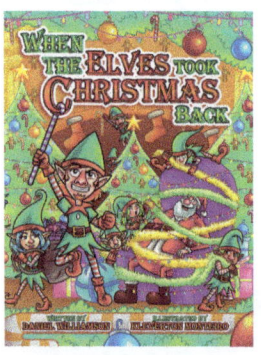

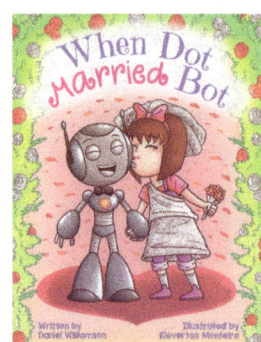

Message from the Author

I'd like to say a massive thank you to every single child and adult that read one of my books! My dream is to bring cultures together through fun illustrations, imagination and creativity via the power of books.

If you would like to join me on this journey, please visit my website danielwilliamson.co.uk where each email subscriber receives a free ebook to keep or we will happily send to a friend of your choice as a gift!

Nothing makes me happier than a review on the platform you purchased my book telling me where my readers are from! Also, please click on my links below and follow me to join my ever-growing online family! Remember there is no time like the present and the present is a gift!

Yours gratefully

Daniel Williamson

@DanWAuthor   @danwauthor   @DanWAuthor

www.ingramcontent.com/pod-product-compliance
Lightning Source LLC
Chambersburg PA
CBHW051251110526
44588CB00025B/2948